The Ultimate Air Fryer Cookbook #2020

Healthy and Delicious Recipes for The Whole Family incl. Vegetarian Bonus

George C. Patterson

ISBN- 9798686426856

Table of Contents

Everything You Need to Know About Your New Air Fryer

Nowadays, we all are more aware of the importance of preparing and eating healthy food. On the other hand, the demand for fried foods has had a recent surge in popularity due to the growing number of fast foods and restaurants all around the world.

It does thus not surprise if air fryers are one of the most popular kitchen appliances. They provide a cheap and healthy way to enjoy fried food at home, with a lower amount of fats.

But do air fryers completely replace any other cooking methods? And what is the best way to use them to ensure that your recipes are always healthy and delicious? In this book, you will find all the answers you are looking for!

How Do Air Fryers Work?

Air fryers work by hot air, which circulates around the food that you wish to cook. This allows the ingredients to cook evenly, creating delicious crispiness.

Because of the action and the power of hot air, you don't need to use too much oil. The hot air will cook the foods, cutting back any excess fat and grease, and leaving it perfectly crispy and tasteful. This also removes all the high-fat and high-calorie aspects that people tend to associate with fried food. In fact, the hot air contains fine oil droplets itself, which take the moisture out of your food, allowing you to achieve the desired crispiness.

Benefits of Air Fryers

If used properly, your air fryer can offer several benefits, such as:

- **Healthier Food.** Since you don't need to use too much oil to prepare your favourite recipes, you will be able to offer your family and your friends delicious food, with a lower amount of fats and calories. To cook your food, you can use either olive oil, avocado oil, sesame oil, or cooking spray.

- **A Safer Cooking Method.** Deep-frying is a cooking method that involves heating a container full of hot oil. This is, of course, a safety risk. However, with an air fryer, even when the oil gets hot, there is no risk of spilling or accidentally touching a hot surface. Nevertheless, you should always store the air fryer out of reach from children, and make sure you use it following the instructions.

- **Reduced Risk of Toxic Acrylamide Formation.** Frying some food in hot oil may cause the release of a dangerous compound, known as acrylamide. This is often linked to the development of cancer. With an air fryer, you can reduce this risk significantly. You can finally enjoy fried food with almost no risks at all. Nevertheless, you shouldn't consume fatty and fried food every day, as this will affect your weight. We always recommended a diet rich in vegetables, steamed food and low-calorie and low-fat ingredients.

Air Fryers vs Other Cooking Methods

Air fryers are the best kitchen appliances to cook deep-fried foods more healthily and quickly. Nevertheless, although they are usually very versatile, they cannot completely replace other traditional methods of preparing foods, such as grilling or baking. It is thus important to understand how to use these machines properly.

In fact, even though air fryers only require a small amount of oil to cook food, they still involve the preparation of ingredients that usually contain a lot more than the usual.

In other words, it is recommended to always lower the oil intake of our daily diets. By consuming fried foods every day or too often, one can increase the risk of heart disease, inflammation and, of course, obesity.

Besides, there are certain foods which cannot be cooked in an air fryer, because of their taste or their texture. If you want to learn more about all the best ways to use your air fryer, and which kind of food you can prepare with it, we recommend checking out all the recipes you will find in this book.

The best foods to put your air fryer to the test

Many people tend to associate the idea of cooking with an air fryer with an unhealthy and fat-rich diet. Nevertheless, there are still plenty of delicious ingredients, including vegetables, which can be cooked with this appliance and still preserve their taste and nutrition.

This includes:

- **Frozen food.** Using your air fryer to reheat or cook frozen food instead of the microwave will make it nicer and crispier. Just like your oven would do, the air fryer allows food to cook more quickly and evenly, but using less electricity.
- **Brussel Sprouts.** Kids and even several adults hate Brussel sprouts, usually because of their texture. You can make them change their mind by cooking your Brussel sprouts with your air fryer, which will help them get crispy and delicious, even with no added oil.

- **Cookies**. If you have some left-over cookie dough in your freezer, you can easily make some delicious cookies with your air fryer. You don't have to preheat it as you would need with your oven, meaning that it will be easier and quicker.
- **Steak**. Yes, you can definitely make steaks in an air fryer, although you may need a bit of practice to find the perfect temperature and cooking time according to the characteristics of your meat.
- **Chicken**. Chicken breasts are healthy, low in calories, and can be used in a handful of recipes. Nevertheless, often they are not juicy enough. You can easily solve this problem by cooking your chicken breasts in your air fryer.

Is every food suitable for Air Fryer cooking?

Although the air fryer is surely a versatile kitchen appliance, there are still a few foods which shouldn't be tossed into it.

This includes:

- **Broccoli**. Not all vegetables are created equal, and broccoli is one of those ingredients which doesn't taste good if cooked in the air fryer. In fact. Broccoli florets tend to get very dry, so you should stick to your usual pan to cook them.
- **Fresh greens**. Kale, spinach and other fresh greens cannot be cooked in an air fryer.
- **Whole chicken**. Chicken breasts are undoubtedly better if cooked in the air fryer. Nevertheless, you should never put large roasts or whole chickens in it. They're too big, and they won't cook evenly in an air fryer.

- **Food with wet batter**. Tempura, corn dogs and other food with a wet batter should never go in an air fryer since they need a proper amount of oil to get crispy.
- **Cheese**. Never put cheese in your air fryer, unless you want to spend the afternoon cleaning a huge, cheesy mess in your kitchen.

Air Fryer: Tips & Tricks

Whether you have never used an air fryer before, or you are looking for a few tips to become a master of air fryer recipes, here you will find all the tricks you will need to enhance your cooking skills.

1. Always preheat your air fryer before cooking your food. You can need to turn it on a few minutes before placing the food inside the basket. This will make your foods crispier and will allow it to cook more evenly.

2. Always follow the instructions. You can enjoy your new air fryer and experiment with all the recipes you want to. However, you must always follow the instruction when it comes to the correct usage of the appliance, including how to clean it up and how to set the temperature. If you notice smoke starting to come out of your air fryer, it may be time to clean it or to check if everything is ok.

3. Grease your air fryer basket with oil or cooking spray. Oils with high smoking points usually work better for air fryers, since they are perfect with very hot temperatures. On the other hand, you should never use non-stick aerosol cooking sprays, since they can cause severe damage to your air fryer.

4. Add water to your air fryer drawer when cooking fatty ingredients. Some foods, such as bacon or pork meat, can be too fatty and thus cause your air fryer to start smoking. Nevertheless, you can add some water to the drawer to prevent this from happening.

5. Check your food while it is cooking. Always make sure your food is cooking evenly, by shaking your air fryer basket a few times during cooking.

6. Place larger foods strategically. You should never overcrowd your air fryer basket. Otherwise, the hot air won't be able to circulate properly and your food won't cook evenly. If you are cooking large pieces of food, you must place them in a single layer and make sure you don't stack them. If you need to cook a large amount of items, cook them in batches.

7. Leave enough room for your air fryer. You should always make sure that there are at least a few centimetres of space around your air fryer, and that you place it on a heat-proof surface. This will help hot air circulate better.

8. Clean your air fryer after every use. It is important to clean the basked and the drawer from any oil and drippings after every use. However, you must never stick any part of your air fryer in a dishwasher, nor use cleaning products which are not suitable for it.

9. Use foil or parchment paper to easily clean your air fryer. If you are going to cook super-greasy food, you can place your ingredients on a foil or parchment paper. This will make your air fryer clean-up easier.

Why You Should Use an Air Fryer

Air fryers are some of the most versatile and easy to use kitchen appliances. Besides, they are particularly sturdy and reliable, since they are made of solid plastic and metal material.

If you are unsure whether you may need an air fryer in your kitchen, there are several aspects you should consider.

First of all, an air fryer allows you to cook multiple dishes at once. This means that if you often find yourself short on time to cook for yourself or your family, with this kitchen appliance your life will immediately be easier. With this machine, you will be able to prepare complete meals within minutes. Because of

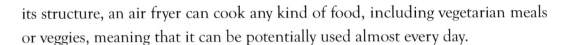

its structure, an air fryer can cook any kind of food, including vegetarian meals or veggies, meaning that it can be potentially used almost every day.

Another important benefit of using an air fryer is that you will finally be able to indulge in fried food, but at the same time you can cut back on fatty oils which are bad for your health and your weight.

If you are concerned about the safety of an air fryer, we recommend choosing one of the latest machines available on the market. They are designed to prevent any of the hazards usually related to hot exterior surfaces and bulky items. All you have to do is to place your air fryers in your kitchen, out of reach for children and pets, and follow the instructions every time you wish to use it.

Although an air fryer may be bulky in weight, these machines are relatively slimmer and, most importantly, smaller than many other kitchen appliances.

In other words, an air fryer is your definitive solution when it comes to finding a fast, convenient and healthy way to prepare delicious meals.

DELICIOUS BREAKFAST IDEAS

Whether you like to indulge in your bed until the very last moment, or you are always in a hurry, cooking your breakfast in your air fryer is the quickest way to enjoy delicious meals without using too many pans and dishes.

AIR FRYER BREAKFAST FRITTATA

DIFFICULTY: EASY ¦ CALORIES: 379.8 ¦ SERVINGS: 2
PROTEIN: 31.2 G ¦ CARBS: 2.9 G ¦ FAT 27.4 G

INGREDIENTS

- 115 g (1/4 pound) breakfast sausage
- ½ cup shredded cheese
- 4 large eggs
- 1 green onion
- ½ red bell pepper (diced)
- Salt and pepper

PREPARATION

1. Cook and crumble the sausages.
2. Combine the sausages with beaten eggs, and all the other ingredients in a bowl.
3. Preheat the air fryer to 180 C (360 F).
4. Grease a non-stick pan with cooking spray or olive oil.
5. Cook the egg mixture for about 20 minutes, or until the frittata is ready.

AIR FRYER BREAKFAST BOMBS

DIFFICULTY: EASY | CALORIES: 305 | SERVINGS: 3
PROTEIN: 19 G | CARBS: 26 G | FAT 15 G

INGREDIENTS

- 3 large eggs
- 3 bacon slices
- 115 g (4 oz.) whole-wheat pizza dough
- 20 g (1 oz.) cream cheese
- 1 tbsp chopped fresh chives
- Cooking spray

PREPARATION

1. Cook bacon in a skillet until very crisp, then crumble it.
2. Add eggs to bacon and keep cooking for 1 minute.
3. Transfer to a bowl and add chives and cream cheese.
4. Divide the pizza dough into 4 round pieces.
5. Place ¼ of egg mixture in the centre of each piece. Wrap it to form a purse and seal the edges with a fork.
6. Cook in your air fryer basket at 175 C (350 F) for 5 minutes, or until golden brown.

HEALTHY VEGETABLE IDEAS

Your family will love your vegetable-inspired recipes cooked with the air fryer. Besides, this can be the best way to show the little ones how delicious their veggies are!

From tender vegetables to roots, including frozen veggies, with your air fryer you can get a result similar to roasting, but crispier and more appealing for the little ones.

AIR FRYER ROASTED VEGGIES

DIFFICULTY: EASY ¦ CALORIES: 37.1 ¦ SERVINGS: 4
PROTEIN: 1.4 G ¦ CARBS: 3.4 G ¦ FAT 2.4 G

INGREDIENTS

- ½ cup diced cauliflower
- ½ cup diced summer squash
- ½ cup diced zucchini
- ½ cup diced mushrooms
- ½ cup diced sweet red pepper
- ½ cup diced asparagus
- ¼ tsp seasoning
- Salt and pepper
- Cooking spray

PREPARATION

1. Preheat the air fryer to 180 C (360 F).
2. In a bowl, mix all your vegetables. Season with salt and pepper, desired seasoning, and oil.
3. Put all the veggies in your air fryer basket and cook for 10 minutes.
4. Serve with your choice of main dish or dipping sauce.

AIR FRYER ITALIAN-STYLE RATATOUILLE

DIFFICULTY: EASY ¦ CALORIES: 79.4 ¦ SERVINGS: 4
PROTEIN: 2.1 G ¦ CARBS: 10.2 G ¦ FAT 3.8 G

INGREDIENTS

- 1 clove garlic
- 1 zucchini, cut into cubes
- ½ large yellow bell pepper
- ½ onion
- ½ small eggplant
- 1 medium tomato, cut into cubes
- Fresh basil, chopped
- Fresh cayenne pepper
- Fresh oregano
- Olive oil
- 1 tbsp white wine
- 1 tsp vinegar
- Salt and pepper

PREPARATION

1. Cut all the veggies into cubes.
2. Preheat the air fryer to 200 C (400 F).
3. Place tomato, bell peppers, zucchini, eggplant, and onion in a bowl.
4. Season with basil, cayenne pepper, garlic, oregano, salt and pepper.
5. Drizzle in vinegar, oil, and wine until the vegetables are well coated.
6. Pour the veggies into your air fryer basket.
7. Cook for 15 minutes, or until tender, stirring often.
8. Let rest for a few minutes before serving.

AIR FRYER MEDITERRANEAN VEGETABLE MEDLEY

DIFFICULTY: EASY ¦ CALORIES: 105 ¦ SERVINGS: 4
PROTEIN: 2.4 G ¦ CARBS: 8.9 G ¦ FAT 7.1 G

INGREDIENTS

- 2 cloves garlic
- 1 small summer squash
- 1 small zucchini
- 30 g (1 oz.) shiitake mushrooms
- 1 cup grape tomatoes
- ½ tsp dried oregano
- ½ small eggplant
- 2 tsp olive oil
- Salt and pepper
- Lemon zest

PREPARATION

1. Cut all the vegetables into slices.
2. Place all vegetables in a large bowl and season with oregano, garlic, and olive oil.
3. Cook veggies in the air fryer at 180 C (360 F) for 5 minutes.
4. Stir well, then cook for further 5 minutes.
5. Sprinkle with salt and lemon zest before serving.

AIR FRYER SPICY GREEN BEANS

DIFFICULTY: EASY ¦ CALORIES: 59.5 ¦ SERVINGS: 4
PROTEIN: 1.7 G ¦ CARBS: 6.6 G ¦ FAT 3.6 G

INGREDIENTS

- 340 g (12 oz.) fresh green beans
- 1 clove garlic
- ½ red pepper flakes
- 1 tbsp sesame oil
- 1 tsp rice wine vinegar
- 1 tsp soy sauce

PREPARATION

1. Preheat the air fryer to 200 C (400 F).

2. Mix the soy sauce, sesame oil, rice wine vinegar, red pepper flakes and garlic in a bowl.

3. Place the green beans in a separate bowl and pour the mixture over them. Let marinate for 5 minutes.

4. Cook the green beans for 12 minutes.

AIR FRYER POTATO WEDGES

DIFFICULTY: EASY ¦ CALORIES: 130 ¦ SERVINGS: 4
PROTEIN: 2.3 G ¦ CARBS: 19 G ¦ FAT 5.3 G

INGREDIENTS

- 2 medium Russet potatoes (cut into wedges)
- 1 tsp paprika
- 1 tsp chilli powder
- 1 tsp parsley flakes
- 1 ½ tbsp olive oil
- Salt and pepper

PREPARATION

1. Preheat air fryer to 200 C (400 F).

2. Mix all the spices together.

3. Season the potato wedge with this mixture, then cook for about 15 minutes.

AIR FRYER ARTICHOKE HEARTS

DIFFICULTY: EASY ¦ CALORIES: 67 ¦ SERVINGS: 4
PROTEIN: 2.6 G ¦ CARBS: 6.6 G ¦ FAT 3.7 G

INGREDIENTS

- 400 g (14 oz.) quartered artichoke hearts
- ½ tsp garlic powder
- ¼ tsp Italian seasoning
- 2 tsp grated Parmesan cheese
- 1 tbsp olive oil
- Salt and pepper

PREPARATION

1. Preheat the fryer to 200 C (400 F).
2. Remove any excess moisture from the artichoke hearts.
3. Sprinkle them with Italian seasoning and Parmesan cheese. Season with salt and pepper, olive oil, and garlic powder.
4. Cook the artichoke hearts in the air fryer for 4 minutes, or until they get brown and crispy.

AIR FRYER BEET CHIPS

DIFFICULTY: EASY ¦ CALORIES: 47 ¦ SERVINGS: 4
PROTEIN: 1 G ¦ CARBS: 6 G ¦ FAT 2 G

INGREDIENTS

- 3 red beets, peeled and cut into 3 pieces
- 2 tsp canola oil
- Salt and pepper

PREPARATION

1. Toss the beets with oil, salt and pepper.
2. Place the beet chips in your air fryer basket and cook at 150 C (300 F) for 40 minutes.

AIR FRYER ROASTED ASPARAGUS

DIFFICULTY: EASY ¦ CALORIES: 94 ¦ SERVINGS: 2
PROTEIN: 9 G ¦ CARBS: 10.3 G ¦ FAT 3.3 G

INGREDIENTS

- 200 g (7 oz.) fresh asparagus
- ½ tsp garlic powder
- ¼ tsp ground peppercorns
- ¼ tsp red pepper flakes
- 1 tsp avocado oil
- ¼ cup grated Parmesan cheese

PREPARATION

1. Preheat the air fryer to 190 C (375 F).

2. Spray the asparagus with avocado oil.

3. Sprinkle with red pepper flakes, grated Parmesan cheese, and garlic powder. Season with salt and pepper.

4. Cook for about 9 minutes.

AIR FRYER ONION RINGS

DIFFICULTY: MEDIUM ¦ CALORIES: 320 ¦ SERVINGS: 4
PROTEIN: 10 G ¦ CARBS: 59.7 G ¦ FAT 4.3 G

INGREDIENTS

- 1 egg
- 1 cup bread crumbs
- 1 cup milk
- Garlic powder
- Paprika
- 1 large onion, cut into rings
- 2 tsp baking powder
- ½ cup cornstarch
- ¾ cup all-purpose flour
- Salt and pepper

PREPARATION

1. Mix the baking powder, salt, corn starch and flour in a small bowl.
2. Dip onion rings into this mixture and set aside.
3. Wish the milk and egg in the remaining flour mixture.
4. Dip the onion rings once again in this batter, then leave them to drain for a few minutes.
5. Place the breadcrumbs in a dish and dip the rings into it until coated evenly.
6. Heat the air fryer to 200 C (400 F).
7. Cook the onion rings for 2 minutes, or until golden brown.
8. Sprinkle with paprika and garlic powder before serving.

MEAT & FISH RECIPES

AIR FRYER RIB-EYE STEAK

DIFFICULTY: EASY ¦ CALORIES: 651.6 ¦ SERVINGS: 2
PROTEIN: 44 G ¦ CARBS: 7.5 G ¦ FAT 49.1 G

INGREDIENTS

- 2 rib-eye steaks
- ¼ cup olive oil
- 4 tsp grill seasoning
- ½ cup of soy sauce

PREPARATION

1. Place all ingredients in a resealable bag. Let marinate for a couple of hours.
2. Remove the steaks from the bag and remove any excess oil.
3. Add a bit of water to the bottom of the air fryer pan.
4. Preheat the air fryer to 200 C (400 F).
5. Cook the meat for 7 minutes. Turn them and cook for another 7 minutes.

BREADED AIR FRYER PORK CHOPS

DIFFICULTY: EASY ¦ CALORIES: 393 ¦ SERVINGS: 4
PROTEIN: 44.7 G ¦ CARBS: 10 G ¦ FAT 18.1 G

INGREDIENTS

- 4 boneless pork chops
- 2 large eggs
- 1 ½ cups croutons
- 1 tsp Cajun seasoning

PREPARATION

1. Preheat the air fryer to 200 C (400 F).
2. Season both sides of the pork chops with Cajun seasoning.
3. Pulse croutons in a food processor, then transfer to a separate dish.
4. Beat the eggs in a separate dish.
5. Dip each pork chop into eggs, then into crouton breading.
6. Grease the air fryer basket with cooking spray and place the chops.
7. Cook for 5 minutes each side of the pork chops.

DRY-RUB AIR FRYER CHICKEN WINGS

DIFFICULTY: EASY ¦ CALORIES: 318 ¦ SERVINGS: 2
PROTEIN: 25.9 G ¦ CARBS: 11.3 G ¦ FAT 18.7 G

INGREDIENTS

- 8 chicken wings
- 1 tbsp dark brown sugar
- 1 tsp garlic powder
- 1 tsp sweet paprika
- ½ tsp mustard powder
- Salt and pepper

PREPARATION

1. Preheat the air fryer to 175 C (350 F).

2. Mix all seasonings in a large bowl.

3. Toss in chicken wings and rub the spices mixture into them.

4. Place the chicken wings in the air fryer basket.

5. Cook for about 35 minutes, or until golden brown and crisp.

AIR FRYER CHICKEN THIGHS

DIFFICULTY: EASY ¦ CALORIES: 213.4 ¦ SERVINGS: 4
PROTEIN: 19.3 G ¦ CARBS: 0.9 G ¦ FAT 14.2 G

INGREDIENTS

- 4 boneless chicken thighs
- 1 tsp smoked paprika
- 2 tsp extra-virgin olive oil
- ¾ tsp garlic powder
- Salt and pepper

PREPARATION

1. Preheat the air fryer to 200 C (400 F).

2. Dry any excess moisture from the chick thighs with a paper towel, then place them on a plate.

3. Combine all the powders together and sprinkle half of this mixture over both sides of the chicken thighs.

4. Cook the chicken thighs in the air fryer basket, skin-side up, for about 20 minutes.

DRY-RUB AIR CRUMBED FISH

DIFFICULTY: EASY ¦ CALORIES: 355 ¦ SERVINGS: 4
PROTEIN: 26.9 G ¦ CARBS: 22.5 G ¦ FAT 17.7 G

INGREDIENTS

- 4 flounder fillets
- 1 egg
- 1 cup dry bread crumbs
- 1 lemon (sliced)
- ¼ cup of vegetable oil

PREPARATION

1. Preheat fryer to 175 C (350 F).

2. Mix the oil and bread crumbs in a bowl.

3. Beat the egg and dip fish fillets into it. Then, dip the fish into the bread crumb mixture until fully coated.

4. Cook for 12 minutes.

5. Serve with lemon slices and your choice of vegetables.

AIR FRYER MEATBALLS

DIFFICULTY: EASY ¦ CALORIES: 95.8 ¦ SERVINGS: 16 MEATBALLS
PROTEIN: 7.9 G ¦ CARBS: 2 G ¦ FAT 6.1 G

INGREDIENTS

- 450 g (16 oz.) lean ground beef
- 1 egg
- 115 g (4 oz.)
- 2 cloves garlic
- 1 tsp Italian seasoning
- ½ cup grated Parmesan cheese
- 1/3 cup bread crumbs
- Salt and pepper

PREPARATION

1. Preheat air fryer to 175 C (350 F).
2. Combine all ingredients together in a large bowl.
3. With your hands or using an ice cream scoop, form the mixture into 16 meatballs.
4. Cook the meatballs in the air fryer basket for 8 minutes.

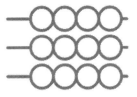

AIR FRYER CAJUN SALMON

DIFFICULTY: EASY ¦ CALORIES: 327 ¦ SERVINGS: 2
PROTEIN: 33.7 G ¦ CARBS: 4 G ¦ FAT 18.5 G

INGREDIENTS

- 170 g (7 oz.) skin-on salmon fillets
- 1 tsp brown sugar
- 1 tbsp Cajun seasoning
- Cooking spray

PREPARATION

1. Preheat the air fryer to 200 C (400 F).
2. Spray the salmon fillet with cooking spray.
3. Combine brown sugar and Cajun seasoning in a bowl.
4. Press flesh side of the salmon into this mixture.
5. Spray the air fryer basket with additional cooking spray and cook the fish for 8 minutes on each side.

AIR FRYER LEMON PEPPER SHRIMP

DIFFICULTY: EASY ¦ CALORIES: 215 ¦ SERVINGS: 2
PROTEIN: 29.8 G ¦ CARBS: 12.6 G ¦ FAT 8.6 G

INGREDIENTS

- 350 g (12 oz.) uncooked, peeled medium shrimps
- 1 lemon
- ¼ tsp paprika
- The juice of 1 lemon
- ¼ garlic powder
- 1 tbsp olive oil
- Salt and pepper

PREPARATION

1. Preheat the air fryer to 200 C (400 F).
2. Combine all the ingredients together in a bowl.
3. Cook the shrimps in the air fryer for 8 minutes, or until pink.
4. Serve with lemon wedges.

AIR FRYER COCONUT SHRIMP

> DIFFICULTY: MEDIUM ¦ CALORIES: 235.6 ¦ SERVINGS: 6
> PROTEIN: 13.8 G ¦ CARBS: 27.6 G ¦ FAT 9.1 G

INGREDIENTS

- 2 large eggs
- 450 g (12 oz.) uncooked, peeled medium shrimp
- 1/3 cup panko bread crumbs
- ½ cup flour
- 2/3 cup unsweetened flaked coconut
- ¼ cup honey
- 2 tsp chopped fresh cilantro
- 1 serrano chile
- ¼ cup lime juice
- Salt and pepper

PREPARATION

1. Mix the flour and pepper in a shallow dish.
2. Beat the eggs in a second dish.
3. Mix panko and coconut in a third dish.
4. Holding it by the tail, drip each ship in the flour mixture, then in egg and finally in coconut mixture.
5. Preheat air fryer to 200 C (400 F)
6. Cook shrimps for about 3 minutes on each side.
7. Meanwhile, whisk lime juice, serrano chile and honey in a small bowl.
8. Serve the shrimps with the honey dip and fresh cilantro.

AIR FRYER "EVERYTHING BAGEL" CHICKEN ROLL-UPS

DIFFICULTY: MEDIUM ¦ CALORIES: 397 ¦ SERVINGS: 8
PROTEIN: 53 G ¦ CARBS: 8 G ¦ FAT 16 G

INGREDIENTS

- ¼ cup bagel seasoning
- 2 large egg whites
- 8 chicken breast cutlets, sliced
- ½ cup sesame seed
- ½ cup chopped baby spinach
- ½ cup shredded cheddar
- ½ cup whipped cream
- ¼ cup chopped scallions
- Cooking spray

PREPARATION

1. Combine the sesame seeds and bagel seasoning in a shallow bowl.
2. Place the egg whites, lightly beaten, in another bowl.
3. In a third bowl, combine the scallions, cheddar and cream cheese.
4. Preheat the air fryer to 175 C (350 F).
5. Spread the cheese mixture on each chicken cutlet, then add 1 tbsp spinach leaves in the centre.
6. Roll up the chicken breasts and dredge in the egg white first, then in the seasoning mixture.
7. Coat your air fryer basket with cooking spray, and cook the chicken for 15 minutes, or until golden and crisp.

AIR FRYER CHICKEN TAQUITOS

DIFFICULTY: MEDIUM | CALORIES: 175 | SERVINGS: 6
PROTEIN: 10.3 G | CARBS: 12.9 G | FAT 9.2 G

INGREDIENTS

- 6 corn tortillas
- ½ cup shredded Mexican cheese blend
- 2 tbsp Mexican-style hot tomato sauce
- 2 tbsp chopped green chiles
- 1 cup shredded chicken
- 1 tsp avocado oil
- ½ diced onion
- 1 clove garlic
- 1 tsp vegetable oil

PREPARATION

1. Fry the onion in olive oil in a skillet.
2. Dd Mexican tomato sauce and green chiles.
3. Stir in chicken and the Mexican cheese blend. Cook until the cheese has melted.
4. Place 3 tbsp of chicken mixture in each warm tortilla. Fold over and roll into taquitos.
5. Preheat the air fryer to 200 C (400 F).
6. Cook the taquitos for 5 minutes, or until crispy.
7. Spry with avocado oil and fry for an additional 2 minutes.

AIR FRYER RANCH PORK CHOPS

DIFFICULTY: MEDIUM ¦ CALORIES: 259.6 ¦ SERVINGS: 16 MEATBALLS
PROTEIN: 40.8 G ¦ CARBS: 0.6 G ¦ FAT 9.1 G

INGREDIENTS

- 4 boneless pork chops
- 2 tsp dry ranch salad dressing mix
- Salt and pepper
- Your choice of serving
- Aluminium foil

PREPARATION

1. Spay pork chops with cooking spray, then sprinkle with the ranch seasoning mix.

2. Let sit for 10 minutes.

3. Meanwhile, preheat the air fryer to 200 C (400 F).

4. Cook the pork chops for 5 minutes for each side.

5. Let rest on aluminium foil for a few minutes before serving.

AIR FRYER SALMON CAKES WITH SRIRACHA MAYO

DIFFICULTY: MEDIUM ¦ CALORIES: 340 ¦ SERVINGS: 4
PROTEIN: 25.5 G ¦ CARBS: 3.6 G ¦ FAT 24.7 G

INGREDIENTS

- 1 egg
- 450 g (1 lb) skinless salmon fillets, cut into pieces
- 1 green onion
- 1/3 cup almond flour
- 1 tsp seafood seasoning
- Cooking spray
- ¼ cup mayonnaise
- 1 tbsp Sriracha

PREPARATION

1. Mix the Sriracha and mayonnaise in a small bowl and store part of this mixture in the fridge while you make the salmon cakes.
2. Add all the other ingredients in the remaining mayonnaise and pulse everything in a food processor for 5 seconds.
3. Form the salmon mixture into 8 patties with your hands. Leave to chill in the refrigerator for 15 minutes.
4. Preheat the air fryer to 200 C (400 F), and spry the basket with cooking spray.
5. Fry the salmon cakes for 8 minutes on each side.
6. Serve with Sriracha mayo.

AIR FRYER CHICKEN PARMESAN

DIFFICULTY: MEDIUM ¦ CALORIES: 251 ¦ SERVINGS: 2
PROTEIN: 31.5 G ¦ CARBS: 14 G ¦ FAT 9.5 G

INGREDIENTS

- 2 chicken breasts
- 1 tbsp grated Parmesan cheese
- 6 tbsp mozzarella cheese
- 6 tbsp breadcrumbs
- 1 tbsp melted butter
- ½ cup marinara sauce
- Cooking spray

PREPARATION

1. Preheat the air fryer to 175 C (350 F).

2. Combine the Parmesan cheese and breadcrumbs in a bowl.

3. Place the melted butter in another bowl.

4. Brush the butter onto the chicken breasts, then dip them both into the bread crumbs mixture.

5. Place the chicken breasts in your air fryer basket and spray some cooking oil.

6. Cook for 6 minutes, then turn and top the chicken with 2 tbsp marinara sauce and half of your mozzarella cheese.

7. Cook for 3 more minutes, or until the mozzarella cheese is completely melted.

8. Serve warm with additional mozzarella on top and marinara sauce to dip.

AIR FRYER MUSTARD CRUSTED PORK TENDERLOIN WITH POTATOES AND GREEN BEANS

DIFFICULTY: CHALLENGING ¦ CALORIES: 286 ¦ SERVINGS: 4
PROTEIN: 25 G ¦ CARBS: 31.4 G ¦ FAT 6.5 G

INGREDIENTS

- 350 g (12 oz.) fresh green beans
- 550 g (1.2 lbs) pork tenderloin
- 350 g (12 oz.) small potatoes
- ¼ cup Dijon mustard
- ½ tsp dried thyme
- 2 tbsp brown sugar
- 1 tsp olive oil
- Salt and pepper

PREPARATION

1. Preheat air fryer to 200 C (400 F).

2. Whisk thyme, parsley, brown sugar, mustard, salt and pepper in a large bowl.

3. Place tenderloin into this bowl and combine until the meat is evenly coated on all sides.

4. Season the potatoes and green beans with olive oil and place into a separate bowl.

5. Cook the tenderloin in the air fryer for about 20 minutes.

6. Leave to rest for 10 minutes.

7. Meanwhile, cook the potatoes and green beans in the air fryer for 10 minutes.

8. Serve everything together.

AIR FRYER BEEF EMPANADAS

DIFFICULTY: EASY ¦ CALORIES: 183 ¦ SERVINGS: 8
PROTEIN: 11 G ¦ CARBS: 22 G ¦ FAT 5 G

INGREDIENTS

- 8 empanada discs
- 1 egg white
- 1 tsp water
- 1 cup picadillo
- Cooking spray

PREPARATION

1. Preheat the air fryer to 175 C (350 F).
2. Spray the air fryer basket with cooking spray.
3. Place 2 tbsp of picadillo in the centre of each empanada disc.
4. Fold empanada discs in half and seal the edge with a fork.
5. Mix the egg white with water, and brush the tops of the empanadas with this mixture.
6. Cook in your air fryer for 8 minutes.

AIR FRYER HOT DOGS

DIFFICULTY: EASY ¦ CALORIES: 270 ¦ SERVINGS: 4
PROTEIN: 9.1 G ¦ CARBS: 23.1 G ¦ FAT 15.2 G

INGREDIENTS

- 4 hot dog buns
- 4 frankfurter hot dogs

PREPARATION

1. Preheat the air fryer to 200 C (400 F).

2. Cook the buns in the air fryer basket for a couple of minutes.

3. Cook the hot dogs for 3-5 minutes.

4. Transfer hot dogs to buns and add your choice of seasoning and side dish.

AIR FRYER ITALIAN-STYLE MEATBALLS

DIFFICULTY: EASY ¦ CALORIES: 122 ¦ SERVINGS: 12
PROTEIN: 10 G ¦ CARBS: 9 G ¦ FAT 8 G

INGREDIENTS

- 150 g (1/3 lb) turkey sausage
- 320 g (2/3 lb) lean ground beef
- 3 cloves garlic
- 1 medium shallot
- 1 large egg
- ¼ cup chopped fresh parsley
- 1 tbsp whole milk
- ¼ cup panko crumbs
- 1 tbsp chopped fresh rosemary
- 1 tbsp chopped fresh thyme
- 1 tbsp Dijon mustard
- Salt and pepper

PREPARATION

1. Preheat the air fryer to 200 C (400 F).
2. Cook shallot and garlic in a medium pan.
3. Combine milk and panko in a bowl and let stand for a few minutes.
4. Add garlic and shallot to the panko mixture.
5. Stir in turkey sausage, beef, egg, rosemary, thyme, parsley, mustard, and a pinch of salt.
6. With your hands, form about 12 meatballs.
7. Cook the meatballs in your air fryer for 10 minutes.

AIR FRYER CORN DOG BITES

DIFFICULTY: EASY ¦ CALORIES: 82 ¦ SERVINGS: 4
PROTEIN: 5 G ¦ CARBS: 8 G ¦ FAT 3 G

INGREDIENTS

- 2 large eggs
- 70 g (2 oz.) all-purpose flour
- 12 craft sticks of bamboo skewers
- 2 all-beef hot dogs
- 1 ½ cups crushed cornflakes cereal
- 8 tsp yellow mustard
- Salt and pepper
- Cooking spray

PREPARATION

1. Slice each hot dog in half, lengthwise, then cut into 3 pieces.
2. Insert a bamboo skewer or craft stick into each piece of hot dog.
3. Place flour in a dish, and the beaten eggs in another bowl. Afterwards, place crushed cornflakes in a third dish.
4. Dip the hot dogs in flour first, then in eggs and, finally, dredge in cornflakes crumbs.
5. Coat the air fryer basket with cooking spray and cook your hot dogs at 175 C (350 F) for 10 minutes.
6. Serve with mustard.

AIR FRYER KOREAN FRIED CHICKEN

DIFFICULTY: MEDIUM ¦ CALORIES: 275 ¦ SERVINGS: 4
PROTEIN: 23 G ¦ CARBS: 61.6 G ¦ FAT 3.6 G

INGREDIENTS

- 450 g (1 lb) chicken wings
- 3 tbsp corn starch
- 1 tbsp oil

Sauce

- ½ tbsp soy sauce
- 1 tbsp brown sugar
- 1 tbsp honey
- 1 tbsp ketchup
- ½ tbsp ginger grated
- ½ tbsp toasted sesame oil
- 1 tbsp gochujang
- 2 cloves garlic

PREPARATION

1. Coat the chicken wings with corn starch and oil. Season with salt and pepper.

2. Spray the air fryer basket with cooking spray or oil.

3. Place the chicken wings in a single layer and cook in the air fryer at 200 C (400 F) for 15 minutes.

4. Meanwhile, you can quickly make the sauce. Combine all the ingredients in a saucepan and bring to a brief boil. Stir well, until you get a thick sauce, then remove from heat and leave to cool.

5. After the first 15 minutes, flip the chicken wings and leave to cook for another 5 minutes.

6. Allow the chicken to cool for a few minutes before serving it with your sauce, a few slices of green onion and lime wedges.

AIR FRYER SWEET & SOUR PORK

DIFFICULTY: MEDIUM ¦ CALORIES: 425 ¦ SERVINGS: 4
PROTEIN: 27.6 G ¦ CARBS: 23 G ¦ FAT 24 G

INGREDIENTS

- 700 g (2 lbs) pork chop cubed
- ¼ cup of sugar
- 2 tbsp corn starch
- ½ onion, chopped
- 1 bell pepper, chopped
- 2 tbsp vinegar
- 3 tbsp ketchup
- 1 tbsp soy sauce

PREPARATION

1. Season your pork shoulder with salt and pepper.
2. Toss the pork with corn starch and place the meat on a baking tray lined with baking sheet.
3. Cook the pork in the air fryer at 200 C (400 F) for 40 minutes.
4. Meanwhile, combine the remaining corn starch with some water, and stir until you get a smooth mixture.
5. Add ketchup, vinegar, sugar and soy sauce to your corn starch mixture. Transfer to a pan and bring it to a boil.
6. When it starts boiling, add your vegetables.
7. Serve the pork with your vegetables and some brown rice.

AIR FRYER SHRIMP SPRING ROLLS WITH SWEET CHILLI SAUCE

DIFFICULTY: MEDIUM | CALORIES: 180 | SERVINGS: 4
PROTEIN: 7 G | CARBS: 19 G | FAT 9 G

INGREDIENTS

- 115 g (4 oz.) peeled shrimp, chopped
- 1 cup julienne-cut red bell pepper
- 1 cup shredded cabbage
- ¼ cup chopped fresh cilantro
- 2 tsp fish sauce
- 1 cup matchstick carrots
- 2 tsp fish sauce
- ¼ tsp crushed red pepper
- ½ cup sweet chilli sauce
- 8 spring roll wrappers
- 2 tbsp sesame oil

PREPARATION

1. Cook the carrots, bell pepper and cabbage in oil in a skillet.

2. Spread on a baking sheet and allow to cool.

3. Place the cabbage mixture, fish sauce, lime juice, cilantro, shrimp and crushed red pepper in a bowl. Stir well.

4. Spoon ¼ cup of this filling in the centre of each spring roll wrapper. Fold the spring rolls and seal the edges.

5. Brush each spring roll with 2 tbsp oil.

6. Cook your shrimp spring rolls in your air fryer at 200 C (400 F) for 7 minutes.

7. Serve with sweet chilli sauce.

AIR FRYER TRADITIONAL FISH & CHIPS

DIFFICULTY: MEDIUM ¦ CALORIES: 415 ¦ SERVINGS: 4
PROTEIN: 44 G ¦ CARBS: 46 G ¦ FAT 7 G

INGREDIENTS

- 4 skinless tilapia fillets
- 2 russet potatoes
- ½ cup of malt vinegar
- 1 cup whole-wheat panko
- 2 large eggs
- Water
- Cooking spray
- Salt and pepper

PREPARATION

1. Cut your potatoes in wedges, coat with cooking spray and cook in your air fryer at 175 C (350 F) for 10 minutes.

2. When your chips are ready, sprinkle with salt and set aside, keeping them warm.

3. Meanwhile, stir together flour and salt in a dish.

4. Whisk the eggs and water in another bowl.

5. Stir together salt and panko in a third dish.

6. Cut each fish fillet into 2 pieces and dredge in flour. Then, tip the fish into the egg mixture and in the panko.

7. Coat each side of the fish fillet with cooking spray and then cook in your air fryer at 175 C (350 F) for 10 minutes.

8. Serve your fish with your chips, and some malt vinegar for dipping.

■□■□■□■□■□■□■□

AIR FRYER MEATLOAF

DIFFICULTY: MEDIUM ¦ CALORIES: 300 ¦ SERVINGS: 4
PROTEIN: 24.8 G ¦ CARBS: 35.5 G ¦ FAT 18.8 G

INGREDIENTS

- 450 g (1 lb) lean ground beef
- 1 egg
- 2 medium mushrooms, sliced
- 1 tbsp chopped fresh thyme
- 1 small onion
- 3 tbsp dry bread crumbs
- 1 tbsp olive oil
- Salt and pepper

PREPARATION

1. Preheat the air fryer to 200 C (400 F).
2. Combine all ingredients together in a bowl and mix well.
3. Transfer the beef mixture to a baking pan.
4. Top with mushrooms and olive oil.
5. Cook for 25 minutes, or until nicely browned on top.
6. Let rest at least 10 minutes before slicing.

■□■□■□■□■□■□■□■□■□

AIR FRYER PORK DUMPLINGS WITH DIPPING SAUCE

DIFFICULTY: CHALLENGING ¦ CALORIES: 140 ¦ SERVINGS: 6
PROTEIN: 7 G ¦ CARBS: 16 G ¦ FAT 5 G

INGREDIENTS

- 115 g (4 oz.) ground pork
- 4 cups chopped bok choy
- 18 dumplings wrappers
- 2 tbsp rice vinegar
- 1 tbsp chopped fresh ginger
- 1 tsp canola oil
- ¼ tsp crushed red pepper
- 2 tsp soy sauce
- 1 tsp toasted sesame oil
- 1 tbsp finely chopped scallions
- ½ tsp brown sugar
- Cooking spray

PREPARATION

1. Cook the bok choy in canola oil in a medium skillet.

2. Add garlic and ginger.

3. Mix the bok choy mixture, ground pork, and crushed red pepper in a bowl.

4. Spoon 1 tbsp of this mixture in each dumpling wrapper. Fold it over to make a half-moon shape and seal the edges with a fork.

5. Grease your air fryer basket with cooking spray.

6. Cook the dumpling at 175 C (350 F) for 15 minutes, or until lightly browned.

7. To make the dipping sauce, stir together soy sauce, rice vinegar, brown sugar, sesame oil and scallions in a bowl. Stir until the sugar is completely dissolved.

8. Serve the dumplings with your delicious dipping sauce.

INDULGENT AIR FRYER DESSERT RECIPES

■□■□■□■□■□■□■□

AIR FRYER BEIGNET

DIFFICULTY: EASY ¦ CALORIES: 88 ¦ SERVINGS: 7
PROTEIN: 1.8 G ¦ CARBS: 16.2 G ¦ FAT 1.7 G

INGREDIENTS

- 1 large egg
- ½ cup flour
- ½ cup of water
- 1 tsp melted butter
- ½ tsp vanilla extract
- ½ tsp baking powder
- 2 tbsp confectioners' sugar
- 1 pinch of salt

PREPARATION

1. Preheat the air fryer to 185 C (375 F).

2. Whisk water, butter, egg yolk, flour, vanilla extract and baking powder in a bowl. Add a pinch of salt.

3. Beat the egg white in another bowl until you get a soft foam.

4. Fold the egg white foam into the batter.

5. Pour the batter to a prepared mould.

6. Place the silicone mould into the air fryer basket and cook for 10 minutes.

AIR FRYER PEACH PIES

DIFFICULTY: EASY ¦ CALORIES: 314 ¦ SERVINGS: 8
PROTEIN: 3 G ¦ CARBS: 43 G ¦ FAT 16 G

INGREDIENTS

- 2 peaches, peeled and chopped
- 1 tsp vanilla extract
- 3 tbsp granulated sugar
- The juice of 1 lemon
- 1 tsp corn starch
- 1 pie crust
- A pinch of salt
- Cooking spray

PREPARATION

1. Drain the peaches, reserving about 1 tbsp liquid.

2. Stir together lemon juice, vanilla, sugar, peaches, and a pinch of salt in a bowl.

3. Mix the peaches reserving liquid and corn starch.

4. Whisk the two mixtures together.

5. Cut your pie crust into 8 circles.

6. Place 1 tbsp filling in the centre of each circle. Fold it over to form a half-moon shape and seal the edges with a fork. Cut 3 small slits on top of each pie.

7. Coat the peach pies with cooking spray and place in your air fryer at 175 C (350 F) for 15 minutes.

■□■□■□■□■□■□■□

AIR FRYER CINNAMON BISCUIT BITES

DIFFICULTY: EASY ¦ CALORIES: 270 ¦ SERVINGS: 4
PROTEIN: 9.1 G ¦ CARBS: 23.1 G ¦ FAT 15.2 G

INGREDIENTS

- 55 g (2 oz.) all-purpose flour
- 1/3 cup whole milk
- 55 g (2 oz.) whole-wheat flour
- 1 tsp baking powder
- 4 tbsp salted butter
- 2 tbsp granulated sugar
- ¼ tsp ground cinnamon
- A pinch of salt
- Cooking spray

PREPARATION

1. Whisk together granulated sugar, baking powder, both flours, cinnamon, and a pinch of salt in a bowl.

2. Cut the butter to pieces and add to the mixture.

3. Combine well and then stir in milk. Keep processing the mixture until you get a dough.

4. Cut the dough into 16 pieces, rolling each of them into a ball.

5. Coat your air fryer basket with cooking spray.

6. Cook the dough balls at 175 C (350 F) for about 10 minutes.

7. Meanwhile. Whisk together water and powdered sugar in a bowl.

8. While the dough balls are still warm, dip them into the powdered sugar mixture to form a glaze.

9. Let cool for 5 minutes and then glaze again.

10. Let cool completely before serving.

AIR FRYER APPLE CHIPS WITH ALMOND YOGHURT DIP

DIFFICULTY: MEDIUM ¦ CALORIES: 104 ¦ SERVINGS: 4
PROTEIN: 1 G ¦ CARBS: 17 G ¦ FAT 3 G

INGREDIENTS

- 1 Fuji apple
- 1/cup low-fat Greek yoghurt
- 1 tsp honey
- 1 tbsp almond butter
- 2 tsp canola oil
- 1 tsp ground cinnamon
- Cooking spray

PREPARATION

1. With a mandolin, thinly slice your apple
2. Coat your apple slices with oil and cinnamon, then with cooking spray.
3. Cook the apple chips in the air fryer at 175 C (350 F) for 12 minutes, or until they are completely crisped.
4. Meanwhile, to make the almond yoghurt dip, stir together the almond butter, yoghurt and honey in a small bowl.
5. Serve the apple chips with the yoghurt almond dip.

AIR FRYER GERMAN PANCAKES

DIFFICULTY: EASY ¦ CALORIES: 139 ¦ SERVINGS: 5
PROTEIN: 8 G ¦ CARBS: 18 G ¦ FAT 4 G

INGREDIENTS

- 3 eggs
- 1 cup all-purpose flour
- 1 cup almond milk
- 2 tbsp unsweetened applesauce
- A pinch of salt
- Swerve confectioners' sugar
- Fresh berries and Greek yoghurt for garnish

PREPARATION

1. Preheat air fryer to 200 C (400 F).

2. Add all the ingredients to a blender and process until smooth. Add more milk if the batter is too thick.

3. Spray your air fryer basket with cooking spray, then pour in a serving of your pancake batter.

4. Cook for 5-8 minutes.

5. Garnish with fresh berries and Greek yoghurt, or honey and maple syrup.

AIR FRYER APPLE FRITTERS

DIFFICULTY: EASY ¦ CALORIES: 298 ¦ SERVINGS: 4
PROTEIN: 5.5 G ¦ CARBS: 64.9 G ¦ FAT 2.1 G

INGREDIENTS

Apple Fritters

- 1 tsp ground cinnamon
- 2 tbsp white sugar
- 4 apples, peeled and chopped
- 1 egg
- 1 tsp baking powder

Glaze

- 1 tbsp milk
- ¼ tsp ground cinnamon
- ½ cup confectioners' sugar
- ½ tsp caramel extract

- ¼ cup white sugar
- ¼ cup milk
- 1 cup all-purpose flour
- 1 pinch of salt

PREPARATION

1. Preheat the air fryer to 175 C (350 F).

2. Grease the bottom of the air fryer with non-stick cooking spray.

3. Mix baking powder, egg, milk, salt and ¼ cup milk in a bowl and stir well.

4. In another bowl, stir cinnamon with 2 tbsp sugar. Sprinkle this mixture over your apples.

5. With a cookie scoop, drop your fritters onto the air fryer.

6. Cook for 5 minutes on each side.

7. To make the glaze, mix all the ingredients together in a bowl. Use to drizzle your apple fritters once ready.

AIR FLAX SEED FRENCH TOAST

DIFFICULTY: MEDIUM ¦ CALORIES: 360 ¦ SERVINGS: 4
PROTEIN: 14 G ¦ CARBS: 56 G ¦ FAT 10 G

INGREDIENTS

- 4 whole-grain bread slices
- 1 tsp vanilla extract
- 2 cups sliced strawberries
- 2 large eggs
- ¼ cup milk
- ½ tsp ground cinnamon
- ¼ cup brown sugar
- 8 tsp maple syrup
- 2/3 cup flax seed meal
- Cooking spray

PREPARATION

1. Coat each slice of bread in 4 pieces.

2. Whisk together vanilla, cinnamon, brown sugar, milk and eggs in a shallow dish.

3. Mix flaxseed meals and part of the sugar in another dish.

4. Dip the bread in the egg mixture and then coat with the flaxseed mixture.

5. Coat your bread pieces with cooking spray and cook in the air fryer at 175 C (350 F) for 10 minutes.

6. Sprinkle powdered sugar and serve each French toast with strawberries, maple syrup.

AIR FRYER STRAWBERRY POP TARTS

DIFFICULTY: MEDIUM ¦ CALORIES: 229 ¦ SERVINGS: 6
PROTEIN: 2 G ¦ CARBS: 39 G ¦ FAT 9 G

INGREDIENTS

- 225 g (8 oz.) strawberries
- ½ pie crust
- ¼ cup granulated sugar
- ½ cup powdered sugar
- The juice of 1 lemon
- 14 g (1/2 oz.) rainbow candy sprinkles
- Cooking spray

PREPARATION

1. Mix together the granulated sugar and the strawberries.

2. Microwave until reduced, stirring halfway. It should take about 10 minutes.

3. Let cool for ½ hour.

4. Roll your pie crust on a floured surface. Cut it into 12 rectangles.

5. Spoon 2 tsp strawberry mixture into the centre of 6 of the dough pieces.

6. Brush the edges with water and top with the remaining dough rectangles. Seal the edges with a fork.

7. Coat your tarts with cooking spray and cook in your air fryer at 175 C (350 F) for 10 minutes.

8. To make the glaze, whisk together lemon juice and powdered sugar. Spoon this mixture over your tarts when they are cool, and then sprinkle some candy sprinkles.

LOW SUGAR AIR FRYER FUNNEL CAKES

DIFFICULTY: MEDIUM ¦ CALORIES: 242 ¦ SERVINGS: 4
PROTEIN: 11.7 G ¦ CARBS: 24.4 G ¦ FAT 16.4 G

INGREDIENTS

- 1 cup almond flour
- 4 tbsp erythritol confectioners' sweetener
- 1 cup Greek yoghurt
- 1 tsp baking powder
- 1 tsp vanilla extract
- 1 tsp ground cinnamon
- 1 tsp almond flour
- A pinch of salt

PREPARATION

1. Preheat the air fryer to 165 C (325 F).
2. Spray the air fryer basket with non-stick cooking spray.
3. Mix Greek yoghurt, 2 tsp sweetener, cinnamon, baking powder, almond flour and vanilla salt. Add a pinch of salt and then, with your hands, make the dough come together.
4. Shape the dough into balls. Cut each piece into 8 equal wedges, and roll each of them in flour, on your working area. Roll each piece of dough into thin ropes and place them into the air fryer.
5. Cook for 10 minutes, or until golden brown.
6. Sprinkle with the remaining sweetener or more cinnamon powder before serving.

AIR FRYER CHURROS

DIFFICULTY: MEDIUM ¦ CALORIES: 88 ¦ SERVINGS: 6
PROTEIN: 1.8 G ¦ CARBS: 16.2 G ¦ FAT 1.7 G

INGREDIENTS

- 2 large eggs
- ½ cup all-purpose flour
- ¼ cup white sugar
- ½ cup milk
- ¼ cup butter
- ½ tsp ground cinnamon

PREPARATION

1. Melt the butter, then pour in the milk and add a pinch of salt.

2. Bring the butter to a boil, and then add the flour. Keep stirring until you get a dough.

3. Let the dough cool for 5 minutes.

4. Mix in the eggs and mix until you get a pastry.

5. With a pastry bag, pipe the dough into strips directly into the air fryer basket.

6. Cook your churros for 5 minutes at 175 C (340 F).

7. Meanwhile, combine cinnamon and sugar in a small bowl.

8. When the churros are ready, roll them into the cinnamon mixture before serving.

AIR FRYER CINNAMON AND SUGAR DONUTS

DIFFICULTY: CHALLENGING ¦ CALORIES: 276 ¦ SERVINGS: 9
PROTEIN: 4.3 G ¦ CARBS: 43.5 G ¦ FAT 9.7 G

INGREDIENTS

- 2 cups all-purpose flour
- ½ cup white sugar
- 2 large egg yolks
- 1 tsp baking powder
- ½ cup sour cream
- 2 tbsp butter
- 1/3 cup white sugar
- 2 tbsp melted butter
- 1 tsp cinnamon

PREPARATION

1. Mix ½ cup white sugar and butter in a small bowl.

2. Stir in the egg yolks.

3. In a separate bowl, mix baking powder, salt and flour.

4. Add ½ the sour cream and 1/3 of the flour mixture into the egg mixture. Store into the fridge.

5. Meanwhile, mix the cinnamon and 1/3 cup sugar together.

6. Roll your dough to form 9 doughnuts.

7. Preheat the air fryer to 175 C (350 F).

8. Brush half of the melted butter over both sides of your doughnuts.

9. Cook the doughnuts in the air fryer for 8 minutes. Brush them with melted butter and dip into the sugar-cinnamon mixture.

■□■□■□■□■□■□■□

AIR FRYER APPLE PIES

DIFFICULTY: CHALLENGING ¦ CALORIES: 496 ¦ SERVINGS: 4
PROTEIN: 3.2 G ¦ CARBS: 59.7 G ¦ FAT 28.6 G

INGREDIENTS

- 2 medium apples
- 4 tbsp butter
- 1 tsp ground cinnamon
- 1 tsp corn starch
- 6 tbsp brown sugar
- 2 tsp cold water
- ¼ cup powdered sugar
- ½ tbsp grapeseed oil
- Milk
- 450 g (14 oz.) package pastry
- Cooking spray

■□■□■□■□■□■□■□■□■□

PREPARATION

1. Combine brown sugar, butter, cinnamon and apples in a skillet. Cook until the apples have softened.

2. Dissolve the corn starch into a cup of cold water.

3. Stir in your apple mixture and cook until you get a thick sauce. This will be your pie filling. Set it aside to cool.

4. To prepare the crust, unroll the pie crust on a floured surface and smooth it.

5. Cut your dough into 8 rectangles.

6. Wet the edges of 4 rectangles of dough and place some apple filling in the centre.

7. Roll out the remaining 4 rectangles, which should be a little larger than the others.

8. Place the bigger rectangles on top of the filling and seal the edges with a fork. Cut 4 small slits in the tops of each pie.

9. Spray your air fryer basket with cooking spray and cook your apple pies for 8 minutes at 200 C (400 F).

Bonus: Vegetarian Recipes

AIR FRYER BAKED POTATOES

DIFFICULTY: EASY ¦ CALORIES: 343 ¦ SERVINGS: 2
PROTEIN: 7.5 G ¦ CARBS: 64.5 G ¦ FAT 7.1 G

INGREDIENTS

- 2 large potatoes
- 1 tbsp peanut oil
- Salt and pepper

PREPARATION

1. Preheat the air fryer to 200 C (400 F).

2. Brush each potato with peanut oil and season with salt and pepper.

3. Place your scrubbed potatoes in the air fryer basket.

4. Cook for about 1 hour or until they reach the desired doneness.

AIR FRYER POP CORN

DIFFICULTY: EASY ¦ CALORIES: 20 ¦ SERVINGS: 4
PROTEIN: 1 G ¦ CARBS: 5 G ¦ FAT 1 G

INGREDIENTS

- 40 g (1.2 oz.) dried corn kernels
- Cooking spray
- Salt and pepper
- Dried chives for garnish

PREPARATION

1. Preheat the air fryer to 200 C (400 F).
2. Spray the kernels with cooking oil and place them in your air fryer basket.
3. Cook for 15 minutes, making sure you check on it every 5 minutes. They mustn't start burning, especially when they begin to pop.
4. When ready, remove from the air fryer, and spray with additional oil.
5. Season with salt and pepper, and garnish with dried chives.

■□■□■□■□■□■□■□

AIR FRYER OKRA

DIFFICULTY: EASY ¦ CALORIES: 120 ¦ SERVINGS: 4
PROTEIN: 1.7 G ¦ CARBS: 6.6 G ¦ FAT 3.6 G

INGREDIENTS

- 170 g (6 oz.) fresh okra
- 1 egg
- ¼ cup bread crumbs
- 1 tbsp olive oil
- 1 tsp flour
- Water

PREPARATION

1. Whisk together the egg and some water.

2. Cut the tops and bottoms of the okra, then slice it into pieces.

3. Toss the okra pieces in the flour, then dip in the egg mixture. Finally, coat with bread crumbs.

4. Cook in your air fryer at 175 C (350 F) for 6 minutes.

5. Season with additional oil, salt and pepper

AIR FRYER PATATAS BRAVAS

DIFFICULTY: EASY ¦ CALORIES: 97 ¦ SERVINGS: 4
PROTEIN: 1 G ¦ CARBS: 15 G ¦ FAT 4 G

INGREDIENTS

- 300 g (10.5 oz.) red potatoes
- 1 tsp garlic powder
- Cooking spray
- Salt and pepper
- 1 tbsp smoked paprika
- ½ tsp cayenne

PREPARATION

1. Boil the potatoes in hot water.

2. Leave them to cool at about room temperature and dry any extra moisture with a kitchen towel.

3. Cut the potatoes into pieces and place in a bowl with garlic powder, oil, salt and pepper.

4. Cook in your air fryer at 200 C (400 F) for 15 minutes.

5. Season with smoked paprika and cayenne before serving.

AIR FRYER GARLIC AND PARSLEY BABY POTATOES

DIFFICULTY: EASY ¦ CALORIES: 119 ¦ SERVINGS: 4
PROTEIN: 2.4 G ¦ CARBS: 20.1 G ¦ FAT 3.6 G

INGREDIENTS

- 450 g (1 lb) baby potatoes
- ½ tsp dried parsley
- 1 tbsp avocado oil
- ½ tsp granulated garlic
- Salt and pepper

PREPARATION

1. Preheat the air fryer to 175 C (350 F).

2. Mix the oil, garlic and parsley together and rub the mixture into the potatoes.

3. Cook the potatoes in the air fryer basket for about 20 minutes.

AIR FRYER GUACAMOLE BOMBS

DIFFICULTY: EASY ¦ CALORIES: 179 ¦ SERVINGS: 4
PROTEIN: 6 G ¦ CARBS: 14 G ¦ FAT 13 G

INGREDIENTS

- 1 egg
- 1/3 cup almond flour
- 90 g (3 oz.) panko
- Cooking spray
- 1 egg white

Guacamole

- 3 medium ripe avocados
- 1/3 cup chopped onion
- 2 tsp cumin
- The juice from 1 lime
- Fresh chopped cilantro

PREPARATION

1. Mix all the ingredients for the guacamole in a bowl.

2. Add the almond flour to make it thicker.

3. Scoop out the guacamole meatballs on a baking sheet lined with parchment paper.

4. Store in the freezer overnight, or for at least 4 hours.

5. Preheat the air fryer to 200 C (400 F).

6. Beat the eggs in a bowl.

7. Spray the guacamole balls with oil, dip in almond flour and then into the egg mixture and, finally into the panko crumbs.

8. Cook the guacamole bombs in your air fryer basket for 8 minutes, or until golden brown. Make sure they don't begin to crack, otherwise take them out of the air fryer.

AIR FRYER ZUCCHINI CURLY FRIES

DIFFICULTY: MEDIUM ¦ CALORIES: 136 ¦ SERVINGS: 4
PROTEIN: 8.6 G ¦ CARBS: 20.5 G ¦ FAT 5.1 G

INGREDIENTS

- 1 zucchini
- 1 cup panko bread crumbs
- 1 egg
- ½ cup grated Parmesan cheese
- 1 tsp Italian seasoning

PREPARATION

1. Preheat the air fryer to 200 C (400 F).
2. Cut your zucchini into spirals.
3. Beat the egg in a dish.
4. In another dish, combine the Parmesan cheese, bread crumbs and Italian seasoning.
5. Dip the spiralised zucchini in the beaten egg first, and then in the bread crumb mixture.
6. Cook the breaded zucchini fries for about 10 minutes, or until crispy.

AIR FRYER CRISPY TOASTED SESAME TOFU

DIFFICULTY: MEDIUM ¦ CALORIES: 445 ¦ SERVINGS: 4
PROTEIN: 23 G ¦ CARBS: 46 G ¦ FAT 20 G

INGREDIENTS

- 400 g (14 oz.) extra-firm tofu, drained
- ¼ cup fresh orange juice
- 1 tbsp + 1 tsp honey
- 1 tsp rice vinegar
- ½ tsp corn starch
- 2 tbsp soy sauce
- 115 g (4 oz.) brown rice
- 2 tbsp chopped scallions
- 1 tbsp toasted sesame weeds
- Salt and pepper

PREPARATION

1. Preheat oven to 100 C (200 F).

2. Drain your tofu with paper towels and place a weight on top. Let stand for ½ hour, then coat it with cooking spray.

3. Place the tofu in your air fryer and cook for 15 minutes at 175 C (350 F).

4. Once ready, keep warm in the preheated oven.

5. Meanwhile, whisk together soy sauce, orange juice, sesame oil, honey, rice vinegar and corn starch in a small saucepan.

6. Bring to a boil, stirring well, until you get a thick sauce.

7. Cook the rice in boiling water.

8. Toss the tofu in your soy sauce.

9. Sprinkle with sesame seeds and scallions, and serve with rice.

AIR FRYER ROASTED CAULIFLOWER

> DIFFICULTY: EASY ¦ CALORIES: 118 ¦ SERVINGS: 2
> PROTEIN: 4.3 G ¦ CARBS: 12.4 G ¦ FAT 7 G

INGREDIENTS

- 4 cups cauliflower florets
- 1 tbsp peanut oil
- 3 cloves garlic
- ½ tsp smoked paprika
- Salt and pepper

PREPARATION

1. Preheat the air fryer to 200 C (400 F).
2. Smash the garlic and mix it with salt, paprika and oil.
3. Rub the mixture into the cauliflower florets.
4. Cook everything in the air fryer basket for about 15 minutes.

■□■□■□■□■□■□■□

AIR FRYER CURRY CHICKPEAS

DIFFICULTY: MEDIUM ¦ CALORIES: 173 ¦ SERVINGS: 4
PROTEIN: 7 G ¦ CARBS: 18 G ¦ FAT 8 G

INGREDIENTS

- 1 can chickpeas, drained and rinsed
- ½ tsp ground turmeric
- ¼ tsp ground coriander
- 2 tsp curry powder
- 2 tbsp olive oil
- 2 tbsp red wine vinegar
- ¼ tsp ground cumin
- Ground cinnamon
- Fresh cilantro
- Salt and pepper

PREPARATION

1. Get rid of the chickpeas skin and smash them in a bowl.
2. Add oil and vinegar and stir well.
3. Add turmeric, coriander, curry powder, cumin and cinnamon. Stir well.
4. Cook the chickpeas in a single layer in the air fryer at 200 C (400 F) for 15 minutes.
5. Once ready, season with salt and pepper, and fresh cilantro.

■□■□■□■□■□■□■□■□■□

AIR FRYER CRISPY VEGGIE QUESADILLAS

DIFFICULTY: EASY ¦ CALORIES: 290 ¦ SERVINGS: 4
PROTEIN: 17 G ¦ CARBS: 36 G ¦ FAT 8 G

INGREDIENTS

- 55 g (2 oz.) Greek yoghurt
- ½ cup drained Pico de Gallo
- ¼ tsp ground cumin
- 1 cup canned black beans
- 1 cup sliced zucchini
- 1 cup sliced red bell pepper
- 115 g (4 oz.) Cheddar cheese
- 4 whole-grain flour tortillas
- Salt and pepper
- Cooking spray

PREPARATION

1. Sprinkle part of the shredded cheese over half of each tortilla.
2. Add red pepper slices, black beans and zucchini slices, then sprinkle the remaining cheese.
3. Fold the tortillas over to form a half-moon shape.
4. Coat tortillas with cooking spray and seal with a toothpick.
5. Cook the tortillas in the air fryer at 200 C (400 F) for 10 minutes, or until the cheese is completely melted.
6. Meanwhile, to make the dipping sauce, stir together lime zest, lime juice, yoghurt and cumin.
7. Sprinkle fresh cilantro over the tortillas and serve with cumin cream and Pico de Gallo.

AIR FRYER ZUCCHINI CHIPS

DIFFICULTY: EASY ¦ CALORIES: 159.5 ¦ SERVINGS: 4
PROTEIN: 10.8 G ¦ CARBS: 21.1 G ¦ FAT 6.6 G

INGREDIENTS

- 1 medium zucchini
- 1 large egg
- ¾ cup grated Parmesan cheese
- 1 cup panko bread crumbs

PREPARATION

1. Preheat the air fryer to 175 F (350 C).
2. Mix the Parmesan cheese and panko on a plate.
3. Cut the zucchini into slices.
4. Dip each slice into the beaten egg first and then into the panko mixture.
5. Place the zucchini slices in the air fryer, trying to not overlap them.
6. Cook for 10 minutes.

AIR FRYER EGGPLANT PARMESAN

DIFFICULTY: MEDIUM ¦ CALORIES: 376 ¦ SERVINGS: 4
PROTEIN: 24.3 G ¦ CARBS: 35.5 G ¦ FAT 15.7 G

INGREDIENTS

- 2 large eggs
- 1 medium eggplant, diced
- 8 slices mozzarella cheese
- ¼ cup flour
- 1 cup marinara sauce
- ½ tsp onion powder
- ½ tsp garlic powder
- ½ tsp dried basil
- ¼ cup grated Parmesan cheese
- ½ cup bread crumbs

PREPARATION

1. Combine all dried ingredients in a bowl.

2. Place the flour in a second bowl and beat the eggs in a third bowl.

3. Dip each slice of eggplant first in flour, then in the eggs, and finally coat with the bread crumbs.

4. Preheat the air fryer to 185 C (375 F).

5. Cook the eggplant slices for about 10 minutes per side.

6. Place the first layer of eggplant slices onto a plate and top with marinara sauce and 1 slice of mozzarella cheese. Repeat with the remaining eggplant slices.

AIR FRYER ASPARAGUS MEATBALLS

DIFFICULTY: EASY ¦ CALORIES: 78 ¦ SERVINGS: 2
PROTEIN: 7.5 G ¦ CARBS: 6.9 G ¦ FAT 3.2 G

INGREDIENTS

- 340 g (12 oz.) asparagus, trimmed and diced
- ¼ cup shredded Parmesan cheese
- ½ cup panko bread crumbs
- Cooking spray

PREPARATION

1. Boil asparagus in hot water for 5 minutes.
2. Drain and let cool.
3. Preheat the air fryer to 200 C (400 F).
4. Mix the Parmesan cheese, breadcrumbs and asparagus in a bowl.
5. Knead the ingredients with your hands until you get a dough.
6. Form some meatballs with your dough and freeze them for 30 minutes.
7. Grease your air fryer basket with cooking spray and cook your asparagus meatballs for 10 minutes.

AIR FRYER SOY-GINGER SHISHIDO PEPPERS

DIFFICULTY: EASY ¦ CALORIES: 36 ¦ SERVINGS: 4
PROTEIN: 1.1 G ¦ CARBS: 6.2 G ¦ FAT 1.2 G

INGREDIENTS

- 170 g (6 oz.) Shishido peppers
- 1 tsp honey
- 1 tbsp fresh lime juice
- 1 tbsp soy sauce
- 1/3 tsp grated fresh ginger
- 1 tsp vegetable oil

PREPARATION

1. Preheat the air fryer to 200 C (400 F).

2. Toss peppers with oil, then cook in your air fryer for 7 minutes, or until blistered and tender.

3. Meanwhile, mix the ginger, honey soy sauce and lime juice in a bowl.

4. When ready, toss the peppers with the ginger mixture and serve warm.

AIR FRYER AVOCADO FRIES

DIFFICULTY: EASY ¦ CALORIES: 319 ¦ SERVINGS: 2
PROTEIN: 9.3 G ¦ CARBS: 39.8 G ¦ FAT 18 G

INGREDIENTS

- 1 egg
- ¼ cup all-purpose flour
- 1 ripe avocado, halved and cut into 8 slices
- 1 tsp water
- ½ cup panko bread crumbs
- Salt and pepper
- Cooking spray

PREPARATION

1. Preheat the air fryer to 200 C (400 F).
2. Mix flour, and salt and pepper in a bowl.
3. Beat the egg with a bit of water in a second bowl.
4. Place the panko in a third bowl.
5. Dip each slice of avocado into the flour, then egg, and finally press into panko.
6. When all the avocado slices are ready, you can spray them with cooking spray and place them into your air fryer.
7. Cook for 4 minutes on each side.

AIR FRYER QUICK & EASY PITA PIZZA

DIFFICULTY: EASY ¦ CALORIES: 229 ¦ SERVINGS: 2
PROTEIN: 11 G ¦ CARBS: 37 G ¦ FAT 5 G

INGREDIENTS

- 1 whole-wheat pita rounds
- 1 small plum tomato
- 30 g (1 oz.) baby spinach leaves
- ¼ cup marinara sauce
- 30 g (1 oz.) shredded mozzarella cheese
- 1 tbsp Parmesan cheese

PREPARATION

1. Spread the marinara sauce over each pita bread.

2. Top with tomato slices, garlic, spinach leaves and cheeses.

3. Place each pita in your air fryer basket and cook at 175 C (350 F) for 5 minutes, or until the cheese is melted and the pita is crisp.

AIR FRYER CORN ON THE COB

DIFFICULTY: EASY ¦ CALORIES: 144 ¦ SERVINGS: 4
PROTEIN: 1.9 G ¦ CARBS: 9.3 G ¦ FAT 11.9 G

INGREDIENTS

- 2 ears corn, halved and shucked
- ¼ cup mayonnaise
- 1 tsp lime juice
- 2 tsp crumbled cheese
- ¼ tsp chilli powder
- Fresh cilantro

PREPARATION

1. Reheat the air fryer to 200 C (400 F).
2. Mix the cheese, lime juice, chilli powder and mayonnaise in a dish.
3. Roll each piece of corn in this mixture. All sides must be covered.
4. Cook the corn in your air fryer basket for 8 minutes.
5. Garnish with fresh cilantro before serving.

AIR FRYER FALAFEL

DIFFICULTY: EASY ¦ CALORIES: 134 ¦ SERVINGS: 3
PROTEIN: 6 G ¦ CARBS: 24 G ¦ FAT 2 G

INGREDIENTS

- 440 g (15.5 oz.) chickpeas
- 3 cloves garlic
- 1 small yellow onion
- 4 tbsp all-purpose flour
- 1/8 tsp crushed red pepper flakes
- 1 tsp cumin
- 1/3 cup chopped scallions
- 1/3 cup chopped parsley
- 1/3 cup chopped cilantro
- 1 tsp baking powder
- Cooking spray
- Salt and pepper
- Hummus, for serving

INGREDIENTS

1. Dry the chickpeas, if necessary.

2. Place the onions and garlic in a food processor.

3. Add scallions, cumin, cilantro, parsley, red pepper flakes and a bit of salt, and then process everything until blended.

4. Add the chickpeas and pulse a bit more (it should be blended but not completely pureed).

5. Sprinkle the flour and baking powder on your batter.

6. Transfer the mixture in the fridge and let cool for a couple of hours.

7. When it's ready, use your hands to form 12 balls.

8. Preheat the air fryer to 175 C (350 F), and cook for 14 minutes, or until golden brown.

9. Serve with hummus, tahini, or salad.

AIR FRYER SWEET POTATO FRIES

> DIFFICULTY: EASY ¦ CALORIES: 120 ¦ SERVINGS: 2
> PROTEIN: 1.1 G ¦ CARBS: 13.5 G ¦ FAT 7.1 G

INGREDIENTS

- 1 sweet potato, peeled and wedged
- ½ tsp garlic powder
- ½ tsp ground sweet paprika
- Salt and pepper
- 1 tbsp canola oil

PREPARATION

1. Preheat the air fryer to 200 C (400 F).
2. Combine all the ingredients in a bowl and the fries are well seasoned.
3. Cook the potatoes in the air fryer for about 10 minutes.

AIR FRYER VEGGIE CALZONE

DIFFICULTY: MEDIUM ¦ CALORIES: 348 ¦ SERVINGS: 2
PROTEIN: 21 G ¦ CARBS: 44 G ¦ FAT 12 G

INGREDIENTS

- 1 small chopped red onion
- 170 g (6 oz.) whole-wheat pizza dough
- 85 g (3 oz.) baby spinach leaves
- 40 g (1.5 oz.) shredded mozzarella cheese
- Cooking spray

PREPARATION

1. Cook onion and spinach in olive oil until the spinach leaves are tender.
2. Stir in the marinara sauce and remove from heat.
3. Divide the dough into 4 round pieces.
4. Add ¼ of the spinach mixture over half of each dough piece.
5. Top with cheese, then fold the dough over to form a half-moon shape. Seal the edges with a fork.
6. Coat your calzones with cooking spray and cook in your air fryer at 150 C (300 F) for 10 minutes, or until golden brown.

AIR FRYER BANANA BREAD

DIFFICULTY: MEDIUM ¦ CALORIES: 180 ¦ SERVINGS: 8 SLICES
PROTEIN: 4 G ¦ CARBS: 29 G ¦ FAT 6 G

INGREDIENTS

- 85 g (3 oz.) all-purpose flour
- ½ cup granulated sugar
- ¼ tsp baking soda
- 1 tsp cinnamon
- 2 tbsp vegetable oil
- 2 large eggs
- 2 medium ripe bananas, mashed
- 2/3 cup plain yoghurt
- 1 tsp vanilla extract
- 2 tbsp toasted walnuts
- Cooking spray
- A pinch of salt

PREPARATION

1. Grease a round cake pan with parchment paper and cooking spray.

2. Whisk together cinnamon, baking soda, salt and flour in a medium bowl.

3. In another bowl, mix together eggs, yoghurt, mashed bananas, sugar, oil and vanilla.

4. Combine the two mixtures, then pour the batter into your pan.

5. Sprinkle with chopped walnuts.

6. Heat the air fryer to 150 C (300 F).

7. Cook the banana bread for 30 minutes, or until browned.

8. Let cool for 15 minutes before slicing and serving.

AIR FRYER GARLIC KNOTS

DIFFICULTY: MEDIUM ¦ CALORIES: 87 ¦ SERVINGS: 2
PROTEIN: 5 G ¦ CARBS: 14 G ¦ FAT 15 G

INGREDIENTS

- 3 cloves garlic
- 2 tsp butter
- 1 tbsp grated Parmesan cheese
- 1 cup all-purpose flour

- 2 tsp baking powder
- 1 cup fat-free Greek Yoghurt
- Chopped fresh parsley
- Salt

PREPARATION

1. Preheat the air fryer to 175 C (350 F).

2. Combine flour and baking powder in a bowl. Incorporate the yoghurt and mix well.

3. With your hands, process the dough until you get a ball.

4. Divide the dough into 8 pieces, then roll each part into a long strip.

5. Tie each ball into a "Knot-like" shape.

6. Spray the dough with olive oil.

7. Cook in your air fryer for 12 minutes, or until golden. There is no need to turn halfway.

8. Sprinkle with chopped parsley and parmesan before serving.

AIR FRYER CELERY ROOT FRIES

DIFFICULTY: MEDIUM ¦ CALORIES: 168 ¦ SERVINGS: 4
PROTEIN: 1.8 G ¦ CARBS: 13 G ¦ FAT 12.9 G

INGREDIENTS

Celery Root Fries

- ½ celery root, peeled and cut into sticks
- 1 tbsp lime juice
- 3 cups of water

Mayo Sauce

- 1/3 cup mayonnaise
- 1 tsp powdered horseradish
- 1 tbsp brown mustard
- 1 tbsp olive oil
- Salt and pepper

PREPARATION

1. Pour water and lime juice over the celery root and let sit for 20 minutes.

2. Preheat the air fryer to 200 C (400 F).

3. To make the mayo sauce, mix all the ingredients together and store in the refrigerator.

4. Drain the celery root sticks, and cover with oil. Season with salt and pepper.

5. Cook the celery root sticks in your air fryer basket for 20 minutes, or until crisp and browned.

6. Serve with mayo.

AIR FRYER "BANG BANG" TOFU

DIFFICULTY: CHALLENGING ¦ CALORIES: 688 ¦ SERVINGS: 4
PROTEIN: 12.7 G ¦ CARBS: 45.4 G ¦ FAT 56.8 G

INGREDIENTS

- 350 g (15 oz.) tofu
- 1 cup mayonnaise
- 1 tbsp Sriracha sauce
- 2 tbsp toasted sesame oil
- 1 cups panko bread crumbs
- ½ cup sweet chilli sauce
- 1 green onion, chopped

PREPARATION

1. Dry any excess moisture from the tofu and leave a weight on it for 30 minutes. After that, cut it into cubes.

2. Drizzle the tofu cubes with sesame oil and let sit for 20 minutes.

3. Meanwhile, you can make the "bang-bang" sauce. Whisk the sweet chilli sauce, Sriracha sauce and mayonnaise until smooth.

4. Place the breadcrumbs in a separate bowl.

5. Preheat the air fryer to 200 C (400 F).

6. Mix the tofu with half of the bang-bang sauce. Coat in the panko and cook in your air fryer basket for 5 minutes.

7. Serve with the remaining sauce and green onion.

AIR FRYER CAULIFLOWER ARANCINI (RICE BALLS)

DIFFICULTY: CHALLENGING ¦ CALORIES: 257 ¦ SERVINGS: 3
PROTEIN: 21.5 G ¦ CARBS: 15.6 G ¦ FAT 11.6 G

INGREDIENTS

- 115 g (4 oz.) riced cauliflower
- ½ cup shredded mozzarella
- ¼ cup bread crumbs
- 2 tsp marinara sauce
- 1 large egg, beaten
- 1 tbsp grated Parmesan
- Cooking spray
- Salt

PREPARATION

1. Cook the cauliflower and marinara sauce in a skillet for 5 minutes on medium heat. Season with salt.

2. Add the mozzarella cheese and stir well until melted.

3. With your hands or with a small spoon, form 6 balls from your cauliflower mixture.

4. Place both the breadcrumbs and Parmesan and the beaten eggs in two separate bowls.

5. Dip the cauliflower balls in the egg first, and then in the crumbs.

6. Cook the arancini in the air fryer at 200 C (400 F) for about 10 minutes. Don't forget to turn them halfway.

7. Serve with additional marinara sauce.

Printed in Great Britain
by Amazon